AF251120

GEORG BASELITZ

NEW PAINTINGS

SEPTEMBER 11 - OCTOBER 10, 1998

PaceWildenstein

32 EAST 57TH STREET NEW YORK CITY

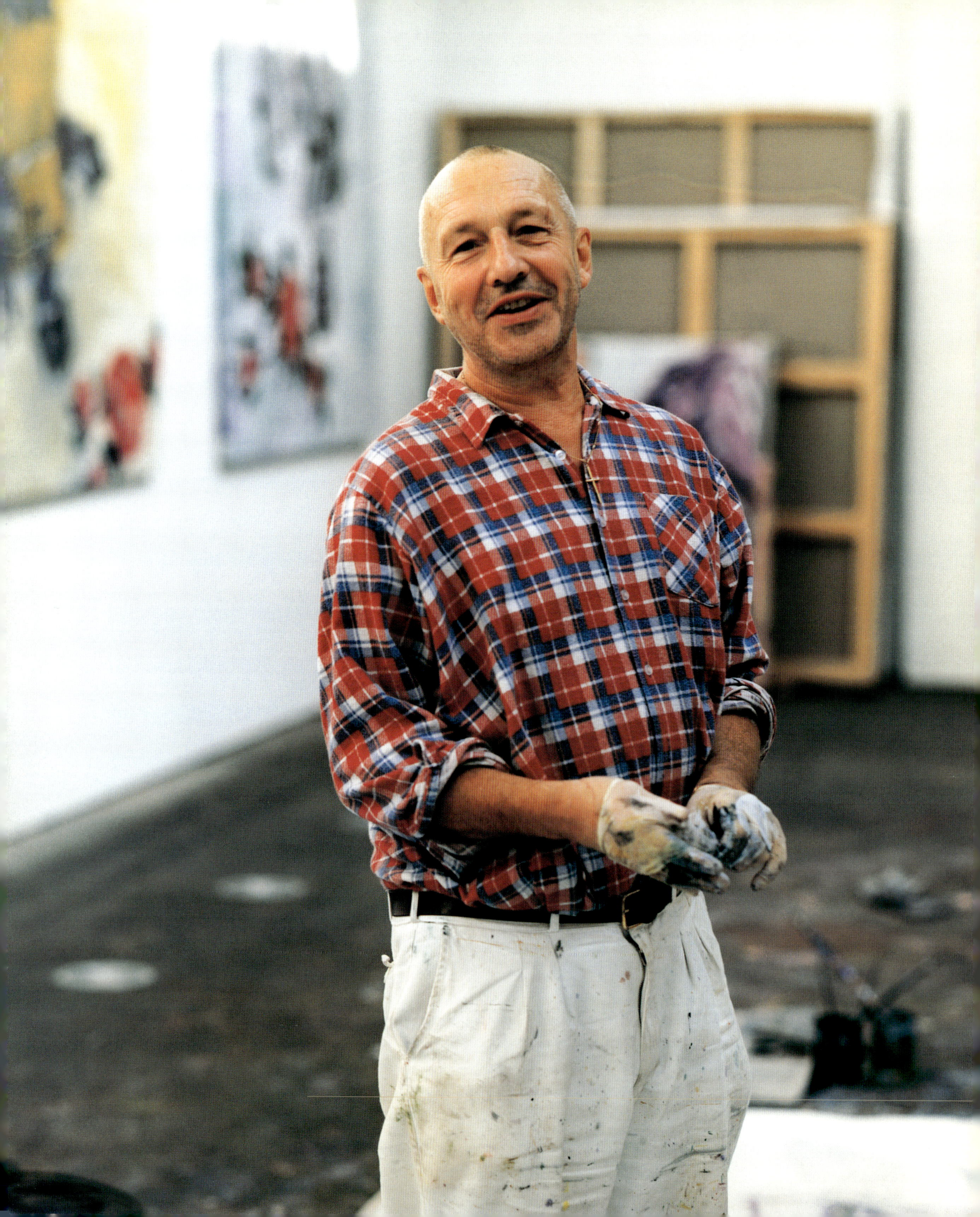

BREAKING LOOSE

A fare-you-well bid abrupt adieu. This is the credo of the intrepid artist, who forsakes hard-won aesthetic peaks, to set sail for uncharted shores. For, only by leaving behind a horizon of things known can he quest after the new pictures within himself longing to be born. No matter how they "look," all of Georg Baselitz's new works are emblems of this departing man. Herein lies the special nature of their achievement, for they are neither "indexical marks" that tell of a performative "self-fashioning," nor iconic clues that call someone into being despite abstracting their identity.[1] Instead, these techniques are used only as departure points in the crafting of a method that draws attention to the pretensions of picture making, so as to do away with dogma once and for all. Indeed, difference is the coat that our man taking his leave wears; it is a mantle that signals a parting of company, long associated with all that is avant-garde.

Baselitz's art is one of pulling away: by distancing himself from a "present past" he begins to draw closer to it so that he can finally cease hankering after it.[2] Such a disposition has both individual and collective dimensions. On the one hand, it describes Baselitz's wish to gaze into the pool of memory, whose surface preserves mirages of his childhood in Saxony. Looking within rather than without, he accesses remnants of experience otherwise blocked from sight, which he then transposes onto the canvas.[3] On the other hand, this frame of mind articulates the relationship of his art to tradition. By soaking up certain well-known motifs and techniques, he innovates, against the undertow of this aesthetic tide, by transforming history's artifacts with the tip of his brush. Both processes entail pushing beyond what a thing once was with the intent of ultimately letting it go. Never mind whether these maneuvers yield personal or aesthetic insights: in order to build the "new pictures" he is after, he first must tackle, dismantle, and take possession of what was formerly inaccessible or the property of others. About this, Baselitz commented more than ten years ago: "When one is able to understand paintings, to look at them, and is a painter oneself, or will at least become one, and thus must experience one's own vitality, then it is simply necessary to destroy all that, as well as all that one loves in order to find other forms . . . . This is a process that takes place in the head and finds its expression on the canvas."[4] And, as it turns out, these tactics remain particularly relevant to understanding Baselitz's most recent work.

To begin with, both their shifting tonality and fluid linearity, which suggest movement without figuring it, refer to certain highlights of postwar American art, including the work of Jackson Pollock. [5] Yet, for all their aqueous, unbroken, and swift, daring strokes, these new paintings are products of neither an automatic nor "get-acquainted" procedure of painting. [6] Rather, as his statement clarifies, Baselitz formulates a concept prior to the act of painting. In them, though handling is everything he never gives into his brush. And though they advocate method as a be-all and end-all of painting, these works attain a schematic plasticity that has more in common with the appearance of certain African sculptures than abstract expressionist painting. [7]

Winterfüße (Winter Feet, 1998, p. 14), for example, is neither conscious of itself as pure surface or paint, nor is it a forthright representation. As such, it all but erases the border between abstract and figurative art. With it Baselitz explores the potential of what he has termed "the run of the line." The outcome is that *Winterfüße* looks like a knitted and pearled painting. Threads of interwoven, swirling pigments weave together a garment that represents man: they *stand in* for the artist as an itinerant, isolated in a winter land of detached aesthetic fabrication. Stroke for stroke, Baselitz builds up an impression of feet that stir to wander at will, backward and forward within time. On perhaps the most obvious level, they forge a link with the footings of his own biography and art, namely the maimed appendages of his well-known *P.D. Fuss* paintings (1960-1963). Amongst these are two titled *Alte Heimat* (Old Homeland), perhaps the earliest indication of Baselitz's preoccupation with his Saxon past. [8]

Then too, the whirling motion of his restless, insistent brush yields a kind of self-portrait that, as in traditional Chinese painting, evinces the aesthetic temperament, rather than the physical likeness, of its maker. Indeed, the oil color of *Winterfüße* has a degree of mobility usually associated with calligraphic art. Both its dynamic color and writhing line prohibit form from becoming fixed, as though it is somehow not "finished." More than this, the painting seems to bellow: Give way!, both as a departing, initially enabled by the stroking oar of the artist's brush, and as an impulse on behalf of the viewer to yield to, and thereby go with, the motif with which one is confronted.

There are no two ways about it: *Winterfüße* solicits its beholder to witness the abstract idea of loss in general, as though it was standing right there before one. Divided even from themselves, these feet, whisked away by the same swipes of paint that construct them, are isolated from a body nowhere in sight. Simultaneously, the ground line from which they dangle bespeaks the forfeiture of an actual horizon, the fragmented condition of a world nearing the end of the twentieth century, from which wholeness has been drained. In sum, the sense of loss, so poignantly evoked by this image is the very one out of which modernism has been constructed for the last century. [9]

Adrift on a canvas raft of his own making, Baselitz paints his way free from the enchanting spell of certain icons of art. Paradoxically, the accomplishment of this feat entails voyaging straight into the eye of the storm. For, if art has a single seductress, then it is surely the female nude and her repeated appearance in a rich history of paintings that cite one another. Baselitz steers clear of this siren by going for its heart, a strategy put into practice in *Ade Nymphen* (Goodbye Nymphs 1998, p. 23).

For one, unlike, say, Pablo Picasso's use of color and line to educe emotional iconic semblance, Baselitz's work continues to be about the impossibility of painted presence. To be sure, the females in *Ade Nymphen* are no more than mere figments, waxing and waning in the same manner as the rushing strokes of paints that attempt to encircle and define them. They come only to go; meaning they head away from the figurative being the brush seems to construct. Baselitz achieves this paradoxical effect by schematizing their thinly brushed bodies to the point that they almost slip off. He then neutralizes their sexuality by proffering them as an obvious variation on a work of art.

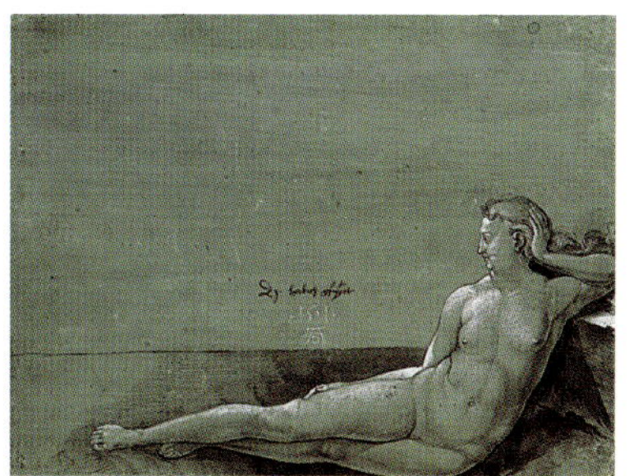

figure 1: **Albrecht Dürer**, *Reclining Female Nude*, 1501
Graphische Sammlung Albertina, Vienna, Austria

As it happens, art, rather than nature, has always been Baselitz's model.[10] And yet, far from the luscious odalisques cited by most painters, *Ade Nymphen* is based upon one of the most masculine nudes ever made within the history of art: Albrecht Dürer's *Liegende nackte Frau* (Reclining Female Nude, 1501, fig. 1). Baselitz's eye was probably drawn to this work because its ambivalent sexuality, combined with its caricatured visage, suggested it as one ripe for transforming. As he once said: "To reinvent painting for yourself, you must address the obvious and the marginal, disrupt the predictable by using what people don't want to look at."[11] In this work, Baselitz brings such an upheaval about by first doubling Dürer's isolated, reserved nude, then schematizing and splashing them with coats of pink color, and finally outfitting them with manes of golden hair. As such, they take on a clichéd beauty that is at radical odds with Dürer's conception of his drawing as a paragon of sublime man.[12]

Of course, parting is inherent to the term "schematic," insofar as it indicates the *reduction* of an otherwise complex idea. To schematize is to turn away from a source so as to move beyond it. Moreover, as has been cogently noted, the process of schematizing in and of itself reveals "the combat of the painter with the past both *around* and *within* himself."[13] Baselitz's painting evinces this exact state: the two nymphs whirl *around* in a dark lagoon as though caught in the vortex of Baselitz's permutations of their forms. Their swiveling bodies also conjure up a storm *within* the painter's head. Sucked down into the cavity produced by this turbulence, they bob up to the surface of the canvas as something finally fingered by him for good. With such maneuvers he subtly demonstrates his ability to do just as well as, if not better, what Dürer boasted was his accomplishment: "Dz hab ich gfisÿrt" (This I have designed), an inscription positioned at the drawing's center, directly above its date and the artist's initials. Baselitz rejoins not only by omitting the phrase, but also by *re*designing the image to testify to the presence of his hand without recourse to the written word. Mocking the perfect proportions of Dürer's nude, Baselitz positions another above her head, ruining the elder artist's symmetrical image. Additionally, he mutates what was once a horizontal composition into a vertical one, as though to say that the beauty of his image is in its ability to hang together as a deliberately arranged axial form.[14] Done with the vanity of names, Baselitz opts for the imprint of authorship left by the circular rims of his "painter's equipment."[15]

The title *Ade Nymphen* is far from coincidental. It both plays with Dürer's consistent use of a monogram (A.D.)—a device he used to authenticate his work—and the fact that his *Liegende nackte Frau* itself is transfigured copy of a "Nymph" made by another artist.[16] *Ade* is not only the phonetic enunciation in German of the initials of Dürer's name but also an antiquated manner of telling someone goodbye. And this Baselitz truly consummates with his painting: with it he bids farewell to an image that Dürer brought to a fare-you-well. Though not exactly one of his most famous works, *Liegende nackte Frau* is nevertheless prized as quite probably Northern Europe's first "constructed" nude, having been generated from measurements and numbers, rather than from a human model. This too would have recommended it to Baselitz, who has long adhered to the premise that "images come into being through construction."[17] A non-semblative drawing par excellence, the work delineates not a woman, but the anatomical structure of ideal man. Baselitz takes this idea a step further in *Ade Nymphen*. For, by making an evanescent version of a nude that now portrays an autonomous disposition that insists—"I am you and you are me"—he literally brushes her off. This is perhaps the penultimate meaning of *Ade*, the credo of our man taking his leave. Finished with the need for a muse, at least here, Baselitz is free to peer unrestrainedly into the deep well of memories imprisoned within him.

No real understanding of his new paintings can be reached without also considering them within the context of his last large series of work (made between 1995 and 1997). Based upon old photographs of his family and himself in Saxony, they represent Baselitz's attempt to conquer and thereby repossess the experiences of his childhood there. For it was in the nourishing ground of first Deutsch-Baselitz and then Kamenz that Baselitz took root as a youngster, underwent the nightmarish experience of World War II, and from which he forever uprooted himself to pursue his calling as an artist. For various reasons, he tends to dislocate much of this to allusions to Dresden, a city in which he spent almost no time at all.[18] Perhaps, because Dresden was the hub of the art world in Saxony and yet merely a small interlude in Baselitz's biography (insofar as its art academy rejected his application in 1955) made it a most viable site for him to displace his aesthetic self in order to come closer to it. Just such a distanced probing is evoked in the painting *Pullover oben* (Pullover On Top, 1997, p. 13). Inspired by a snapshot taken when he was about eight years of age, Baselitz depicts himself with his own doppelgänger. The gesture of his right self tugging at his ear suggests an attempt to hear the sounds of a past long since stilled, including what he had been told as a child about the thunderous destruction of Dresden on 1 May 1945. The boy's wide-open eyes, filled with the white of fright and a grimace, forced into a strained grin, make apparent the turmoil he must have undergone during those war years.

The same strategy—splitting an image of the self as a distancing that enables nearing—is taken several degrees further in many of Baselitz's newer paintings. In them, Baselitz is both in and out of the picture, concealed at times beneath an image of a vulnerable, anonymous child, who drifts about in the realm of dream. *Knaben Hinterglas* (Boy Behind Glass, 1998, p. 21) is really a self-portrait, but one that, except for the large ear and a pouty countenance, is almost entirely hidden behind a borrowed motif from

Schlafender Knabe (Sleeping Boy, 1802), an obscure work, by the nineteenth-century Dresden artist, Caspar David Friedrich. Baselitz's selection of an inked work of art bears witness once more to his present preoccupation with making paintings whose line has a power heretofore the preserve of drawing.

Coincidentally or not, the word *Hinterglas* (reverse-glass painting) alludes to a technique mastered by certain Slovakian folk artists, whose works of art Baselitz often saw as a child. Like a reverse-glass painting, Baselitz's is not only schematic but infused with a mysterious luminosity. Gone is the restrained, lofty quality of Friedrich's rendering. In its place, is an image that pulsates with an enchanted vital life, as though it dreamt itself into being. Floating around in a globule of pink color, the fluid matrix of motherland nurtures this musing child. Firmly lodged in her soil, like a seed in a womb, Baselitz engenders art. In the painting, the fruits of his labor—the black bosom-like plums between which he hovers—also stand ready to suckle him. Birthed by the genius of a mother, who is in the midst of dissolving from sight, he pursues the attainment of genius as a self that is Other.

Abandoned to the concrete world at large, Baselitz divides from himself in order to get at the heart of all that he is. Pregnant with memories generated by the sequestering mantle of reverie, he oozes with the lifeblood of painting. Here then, departing man is emblematized as a castaway. And indeed, the aqueous placenta in which Baselitz is still housed is already beginning to recede. Throbbing to the rhythm of a pulling away that is an incessant birth, he "passes over," as it were, without loss.[19] Done with waiting, breaking loose, and leaving, he catches sight of himself as never before. The image also lets its beholder glimpse the very essence of what makes painting possible: the invention of a self-contained space of abandoned being, whose madly beating heart bestows upon the world gifts of art.

Pamela Kort
Los Angeles, 12 August 1998

Pamela Kort, PhD, is an art historian specializing in twentieth century art of German speaking Europe. She lives and works in Cologne and Los Angeles. She is the author of numerous catalogue essays on Baselitz, Beuys, and Immendorff and is writing a forthcoming book on the revival of painting in post World War II Germany.

[1] For a discussion of "indexicality," see Richard Schiff, "Performing an Appearance: On the Surface of Abstract Expressionism," in <u>Abstract Expressionism: The Critical Developments</u>, exh. cat. (Buffalo: Albright-Knox Art Gallery, 19 September-29 November 1987), 94-123. On "iconic" semblance, see William Rubin, "Reflections on Picasso and Portraiture," in <u>Picasso and Portraiture: Representation and Transformation</u>, exh. cat. (New York: Museum of Modern Art, 28 April-17 September 1996), 13-110.

[2] See Richard Terdiman, <u>Present Past: Modernity and the Memory Crisis</u> (Ithaca: Cornell University Press, 1993).

[3] Pamela Kort, "The Painting of Preservation," in <u>Baselitz: Wir besuchen den Rhein</u>, exh. cat. (Dresden: Dresdner Kunstverein 26 April-22 June 1997), 66-75.

[4] On Baselitz's aspiration (at least since 1979) to make a "new picture," see Ulrich Weisner, "Wechselbeziehungen im Prozess der Kunst: Nach einem Gespräch mit Georg Baselitz," in <u>Georg Baselitz: Vier Wände</u>, exh. cat. (Bielefeld: Kunsthalle, 1 September-27 October 1985), 20. See also Georg Baselitz, cited in Weisner, 23 (all translations are by the author).

[5] Baselitz first encountered the work of these American painters as a student in Fall of 1958 in Berlin, where he saw the exhibitions "The New American Painting" and "Jackson Pollock: 1912-1956." See Diane Waldman, <u>Georg Baselitz</u>, exh. cat. (New York: Guggenheim Museum, 1995), 15-16.

[6] Jackson Pollock, "My Painting," in <u>Possibilities 1: An Occasional Review</u> (Winter 1947-48), cited in Jonathan Fineberg, <u>Art Since 1940: Strategies of Being</u> (New York: Harry N. Abrams, 1995), 96.

[7] See Daniel P. Biebuyck, "Schemata in Lega Art," in <u>Form in Indigenous Art: Schematisation in the Art of Aboriginal Australia and Prehistoric Europe</u>, ed. Peter J. Ucko (London: Gerald Duckworth and Co., Ltd., 1977), 59-65.

[8] Georg Baselitz, conversation with the author, 21 February 1997. "My painting has always had very much to do with remembering, with experience, and above all with other paintings . . . with the history of my painting." Baselitz's <u>P.D. Fuss</u> works are illustrated in <u>Georg Baselitz: Der Weg der Erfindung</u>, exh. cat. (Frankfurt am Main: Städelschen Kunstinstitut, 5 May-14 August 1988), 120-121.

[9] Linda Nochlin, <u>The Body in Pieces: The Fragment as a Metaphor of Modernity</u> (London: Thames and Hudson, 1994).

[10] See Weisner, 13. See also Georg Baselitz, cited in Weisner, 13: "I do not see the world at all, but works of art, no matter in which universe they came into existence."

[11] Georg Baselitz, cited in Michael Auping, <u>Georg Baselitz: Portraits of Elke</u>, exh. cat. (Fort Worth: Museum of Modern Art, 26 October 1997-25 January 1998), 21.

[12] Joseph Leo Koerner, <u>The Moment of Self-Portraiture in German Renaissance Art</u> (Chicago: University of Chicago Press, 1993), 189.

13   Norman Bryson, <u>Tradition and Desire: From David to Delacroix</u> (Cambridge: Cambridge University Press, 1984), 19.

14   Rosalind Krauss, <u>Cindy Sherman, 1975-1993</u>, 1993 cited in Nochlin, 21.

15   See Georg Baselitz, "Painter's Equipment," 1985 reprinted in Waldman, 216-220.

16   See Walter Koschatzky and Alice Strobl, <u>Dürer Drawings in the Albertina</u>, trans. Heide and Alastair Grieve (Greenwich, Conn.: New York Graphic Society Ltd., 1972), 8. "[Dürer] based the figure on a specific model: a picture of a Nymph, attributed to Mantegna, which only survives in an engraving by Marcantonio Raimondi."

17   Georg Baselitz, cited in Wiesner, 13: "Paintings come into existence as a result of constructions."

18   Werner Schade, "The First and the Best Pictures," in <u>Baselitz: Wir besuchen den Rhein</u>, 122-123.

19   Jean-Luc Nancy, <u>The Birth to Presence</u>, trans. Brian Holmes (Stanford: Stanford University Press, 1993), 13; 32-34.

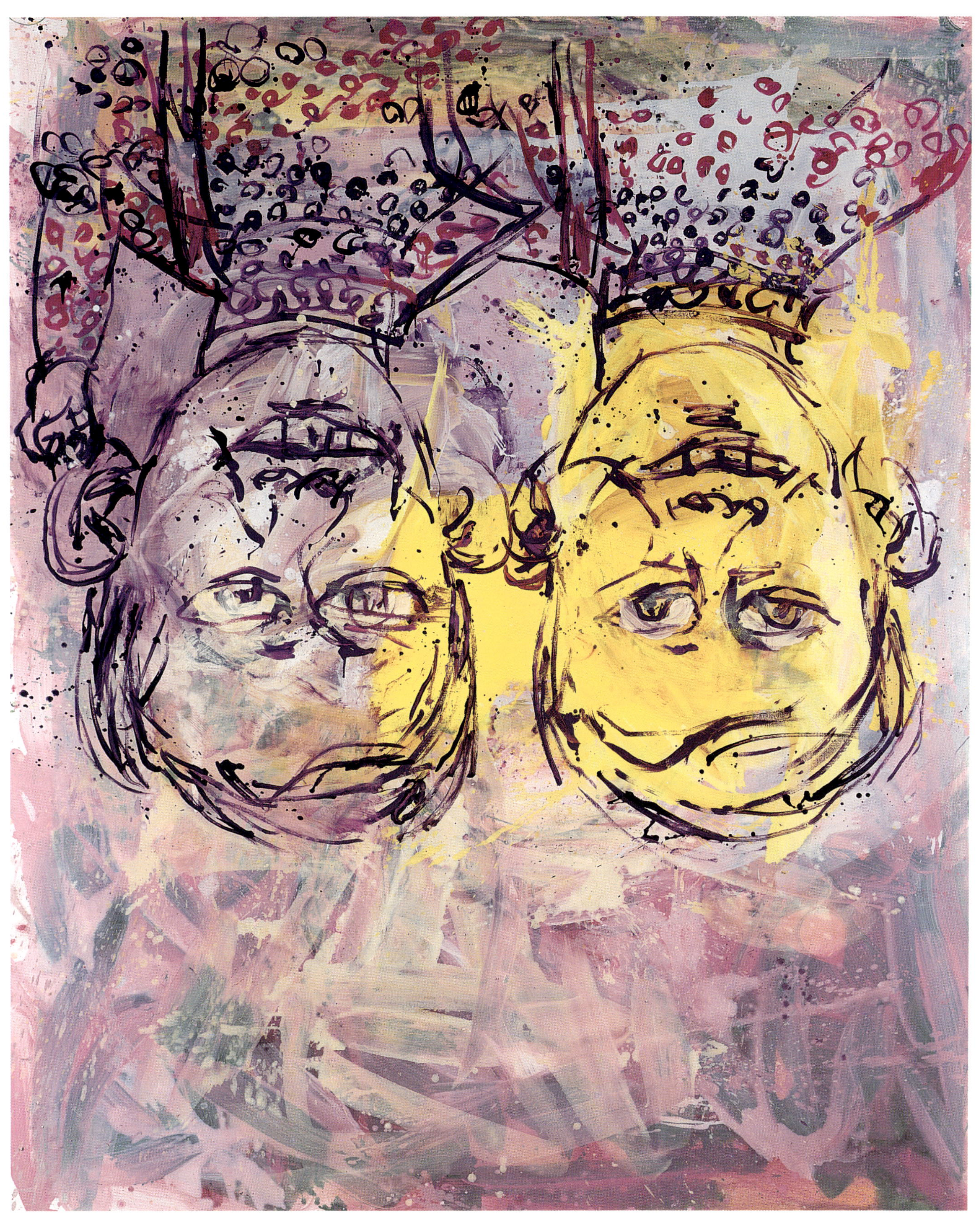

PULLOVER OBEN

May 2–15, 1997
oil on canvas, 98 ½ x 78 ¾"

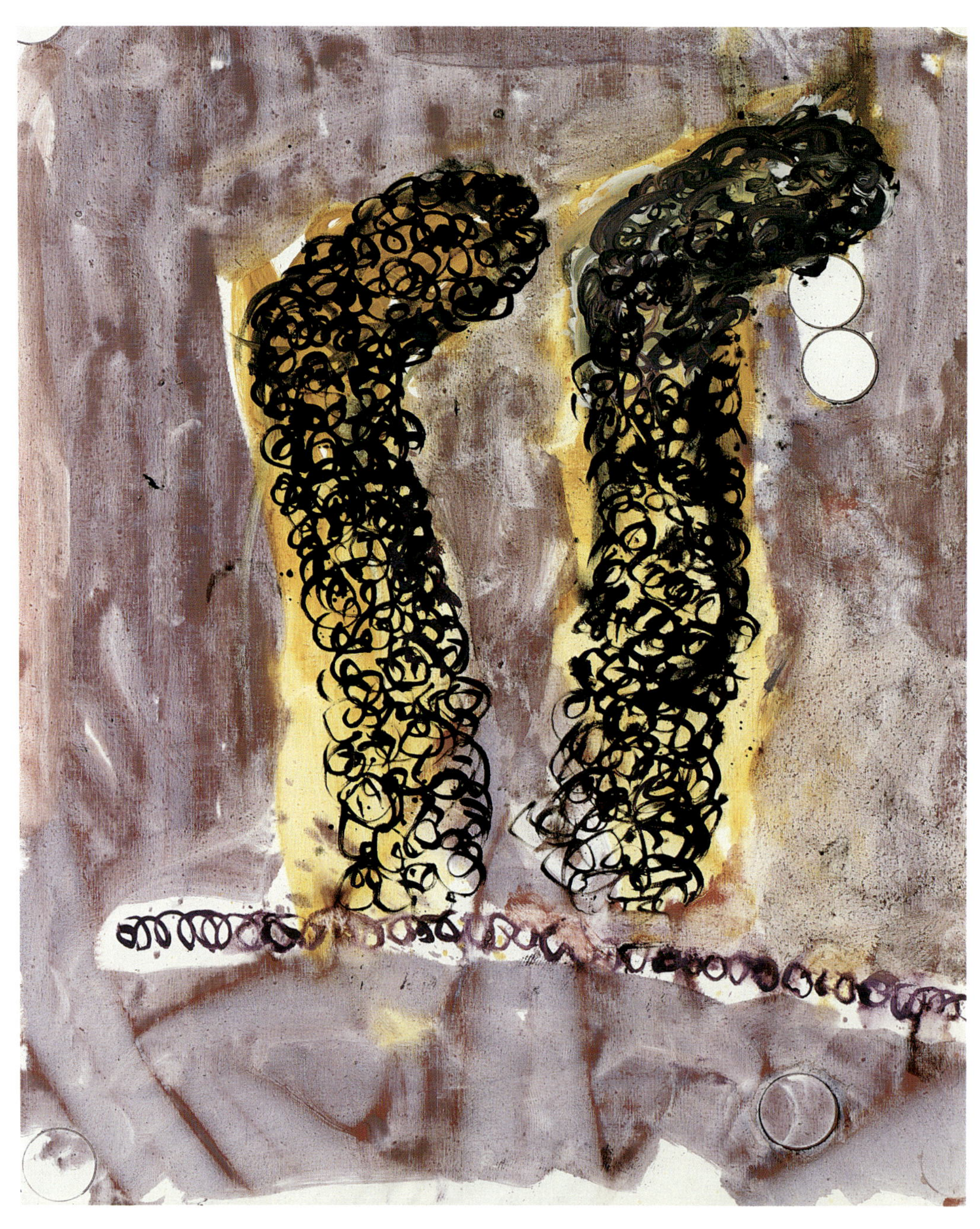

WINTERFÜßE

January 6-7, 1998
oil on canvas, 63 ¾ x 51 ¼″

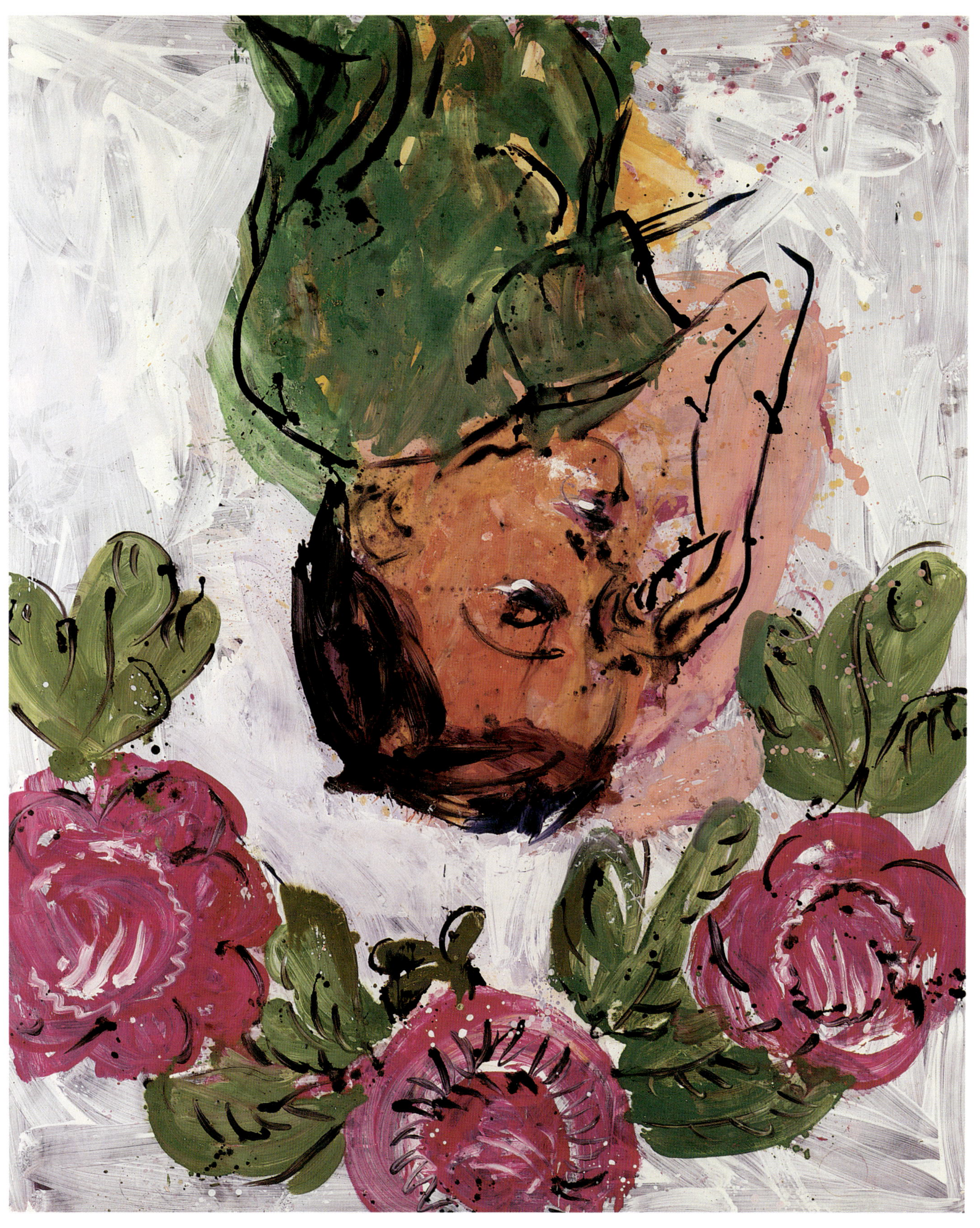

June 2 - July 25, 1997
oil on canvas, 98 ½ x 78 ¾ ˝

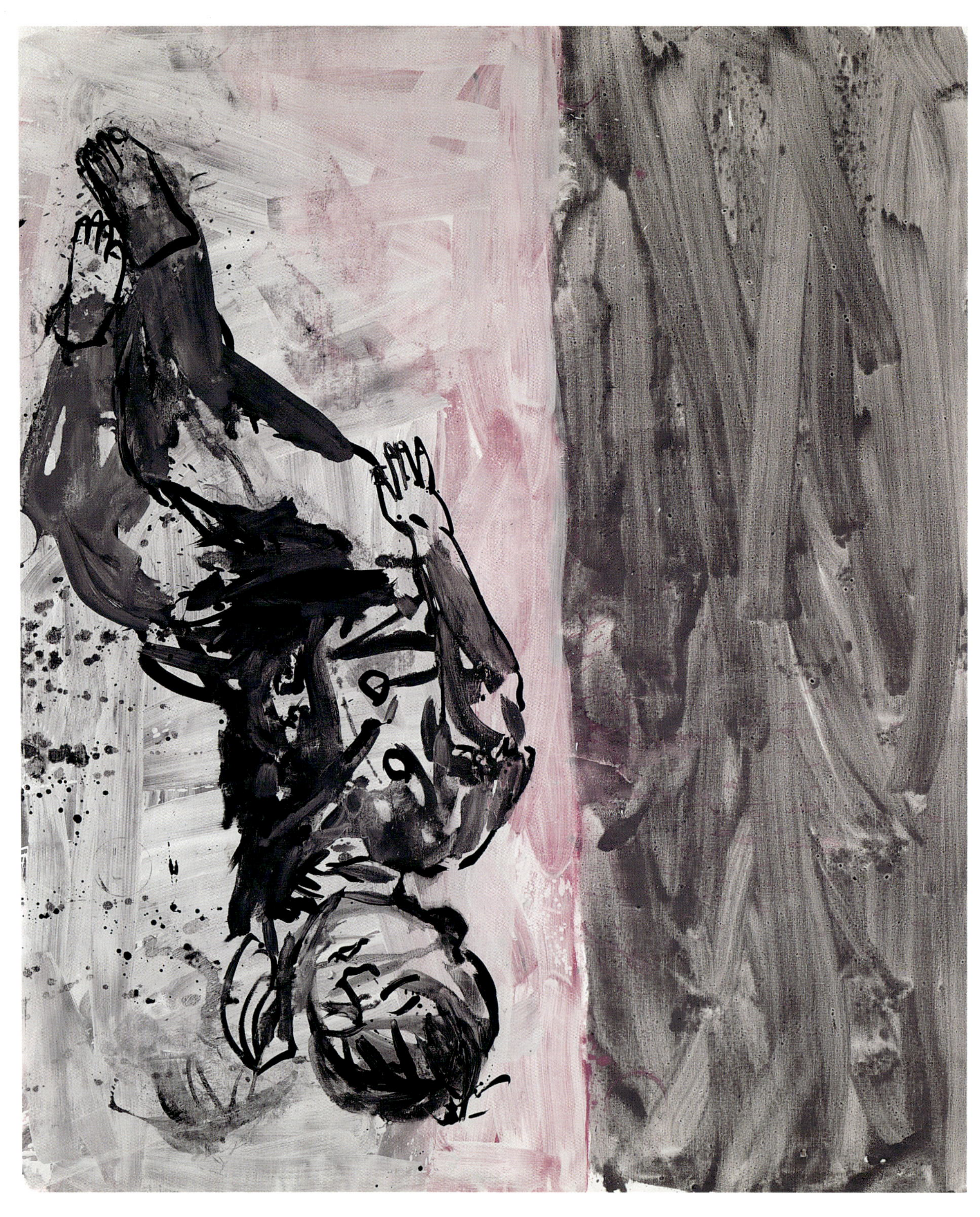

KNABEN II

April 3-6, 1998
oil on canvas, 78 ¾ x 63 ¾″

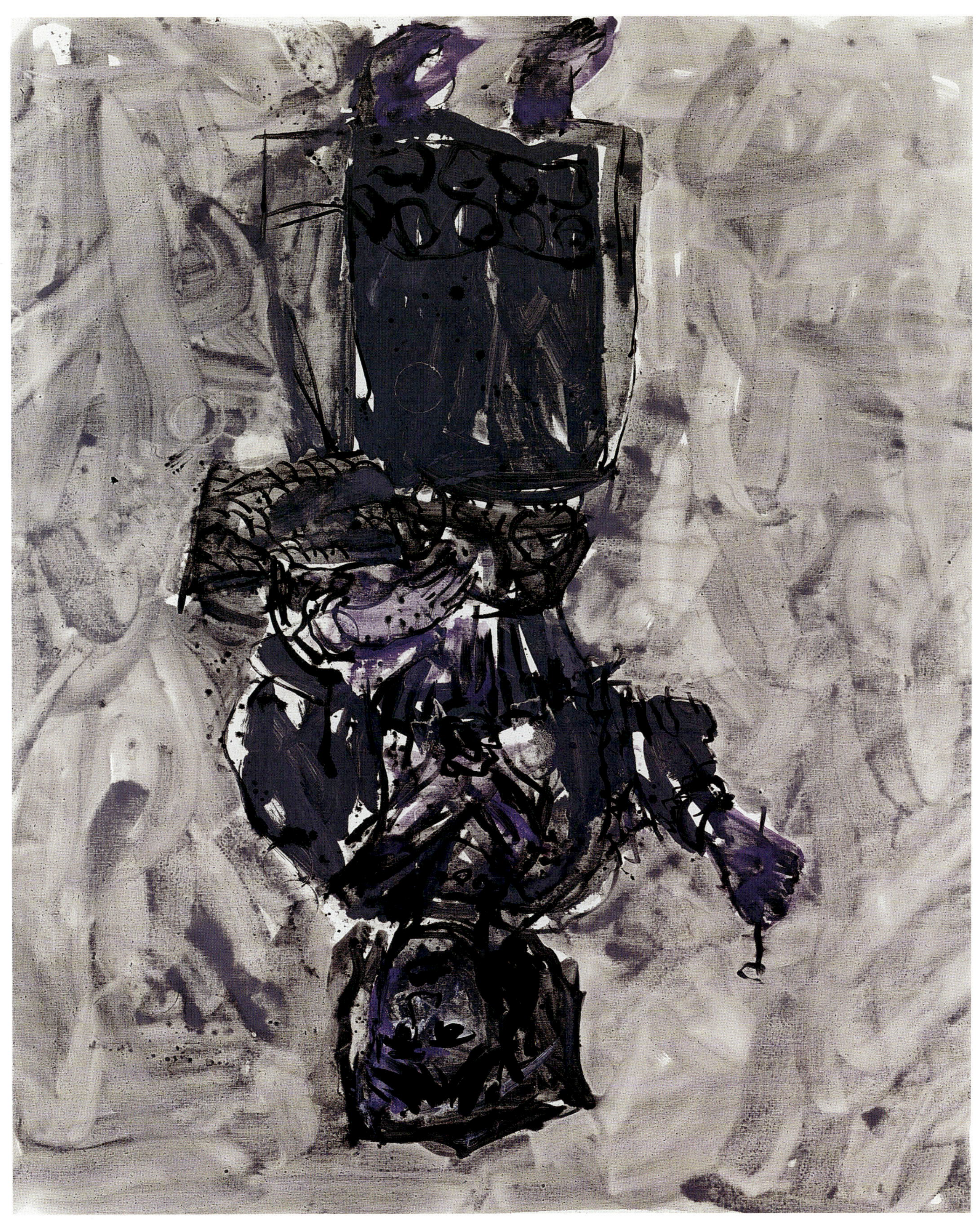

Die Italienerin mit Blume

February 25, 1998
oil on canvas, 98 ½ x 78 ¾″

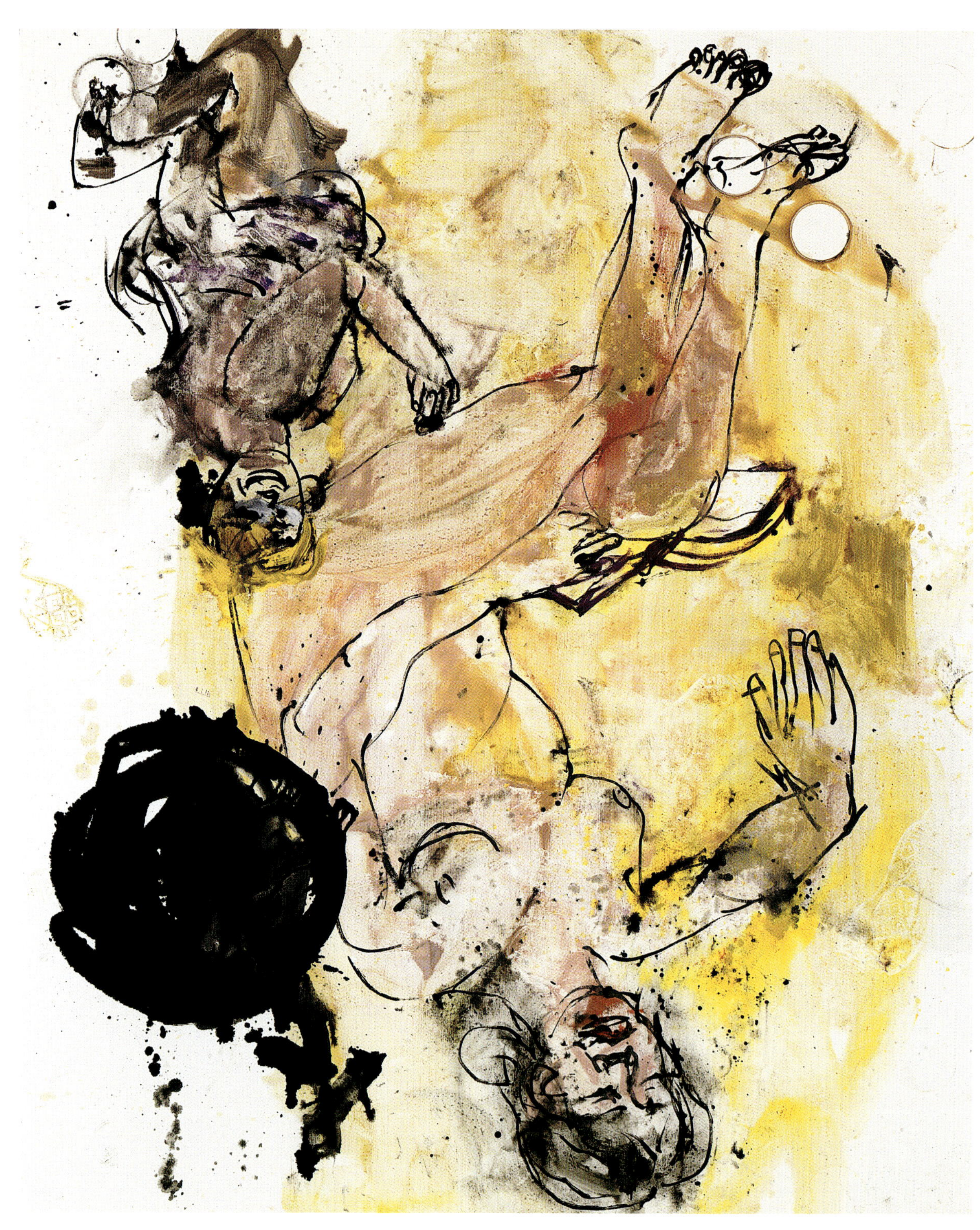

Lesende Mutter

May 29-30, 1998
oil on canvas, 79 ½ x 63 ¾"

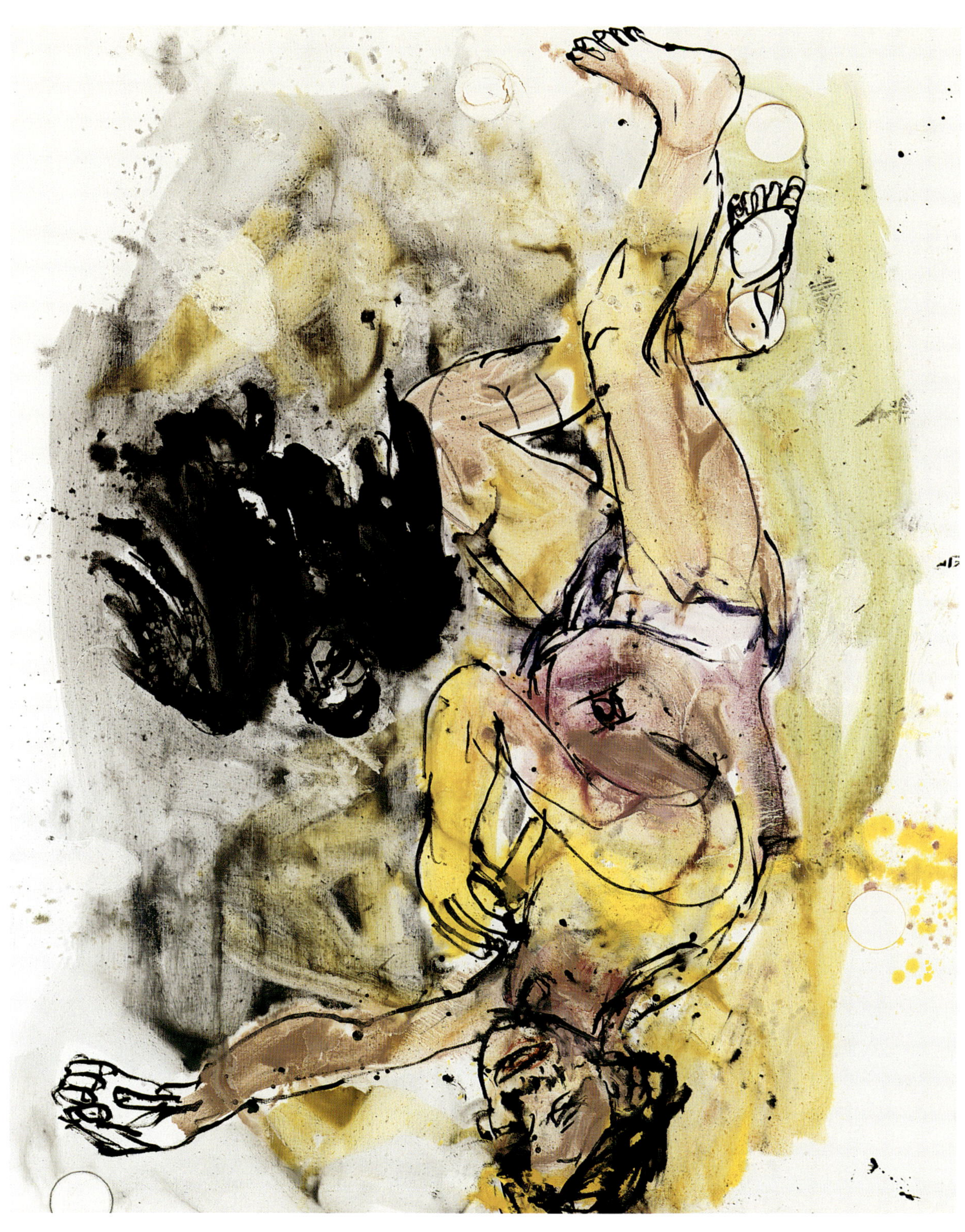

May 29 - June 1, 1998
oil on canvas, 79 ½ x 63 ¾″

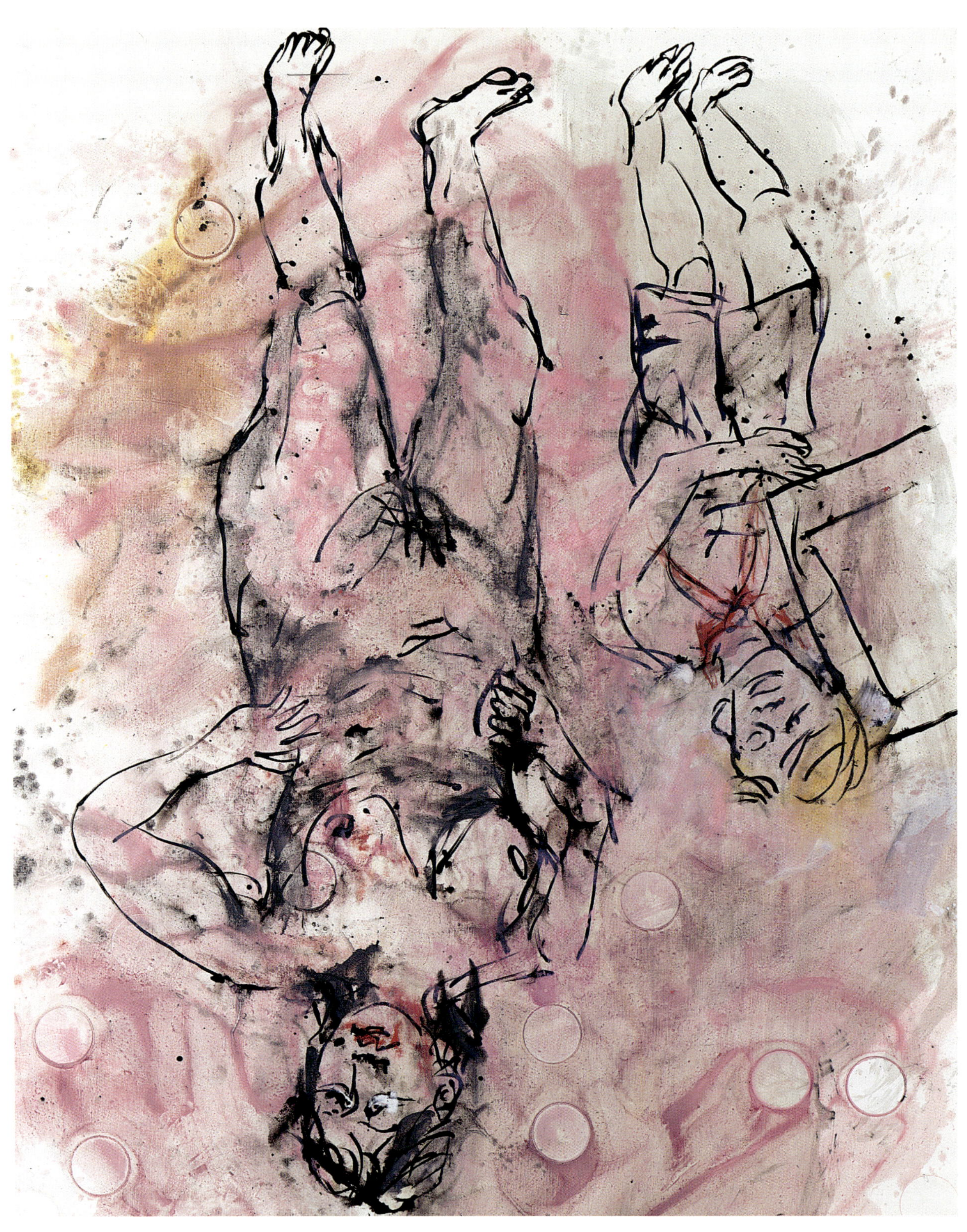

LAKTIONOV DIE NEUE WOHNUNG

June 4-7, 1998
oil on canvas, 80 x 63¾″

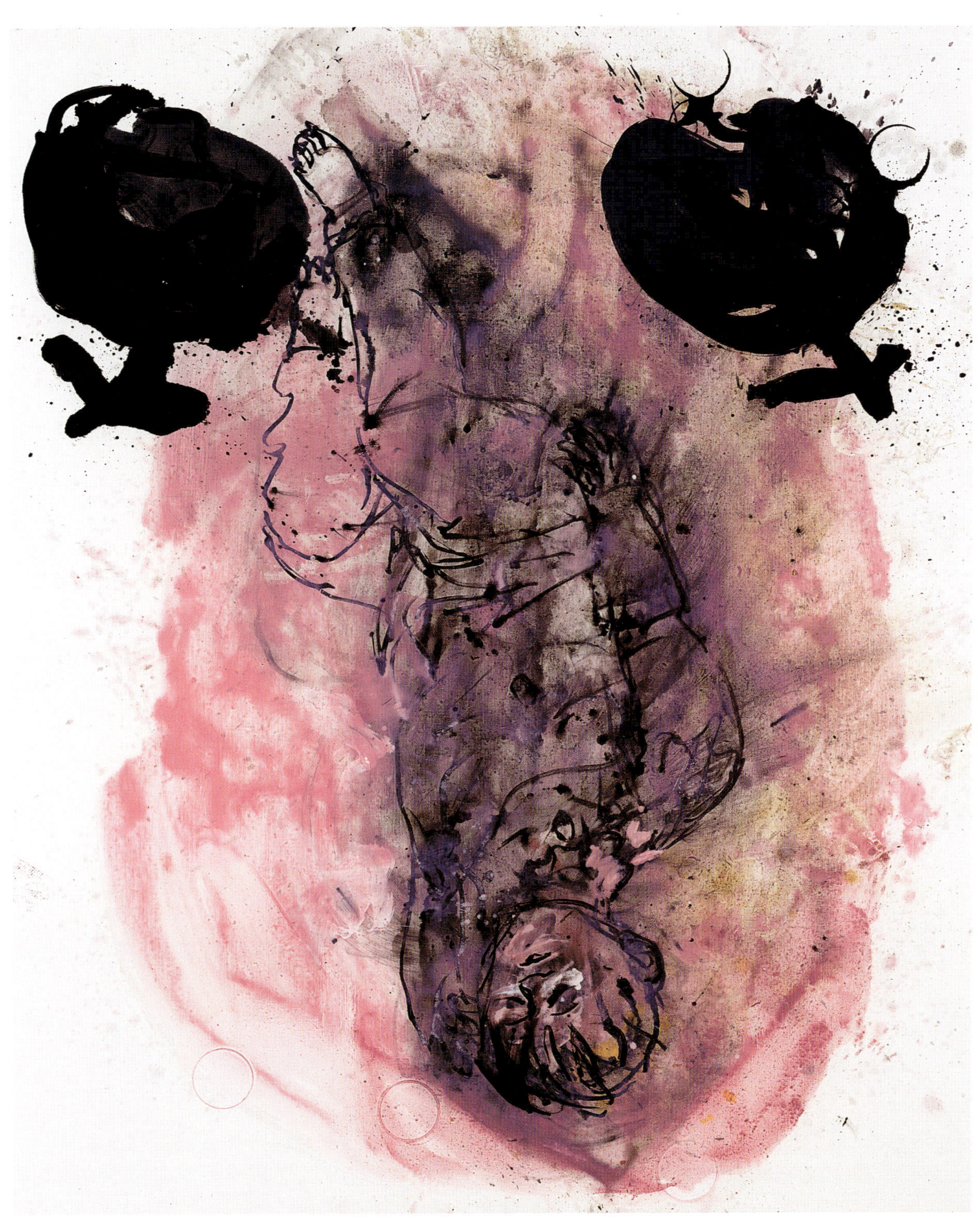

KNABEN HINTERGLAS

June 9, 1998
oil on canvas, 78 ¾ x 63 ¾″

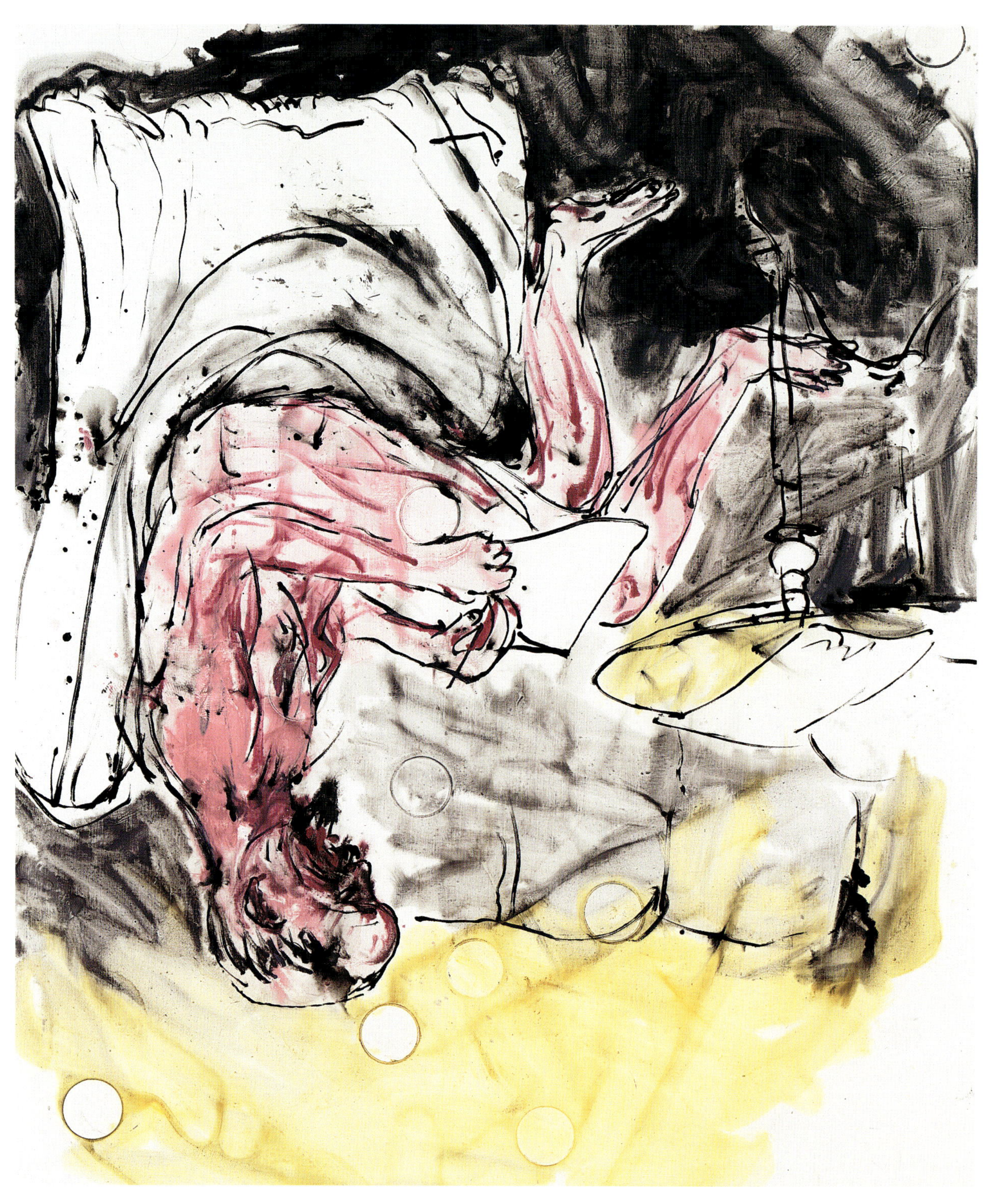

LENIN IM SMOLNY I

June 9, 1998
oil on canvas, 78 ¾ x 65˝

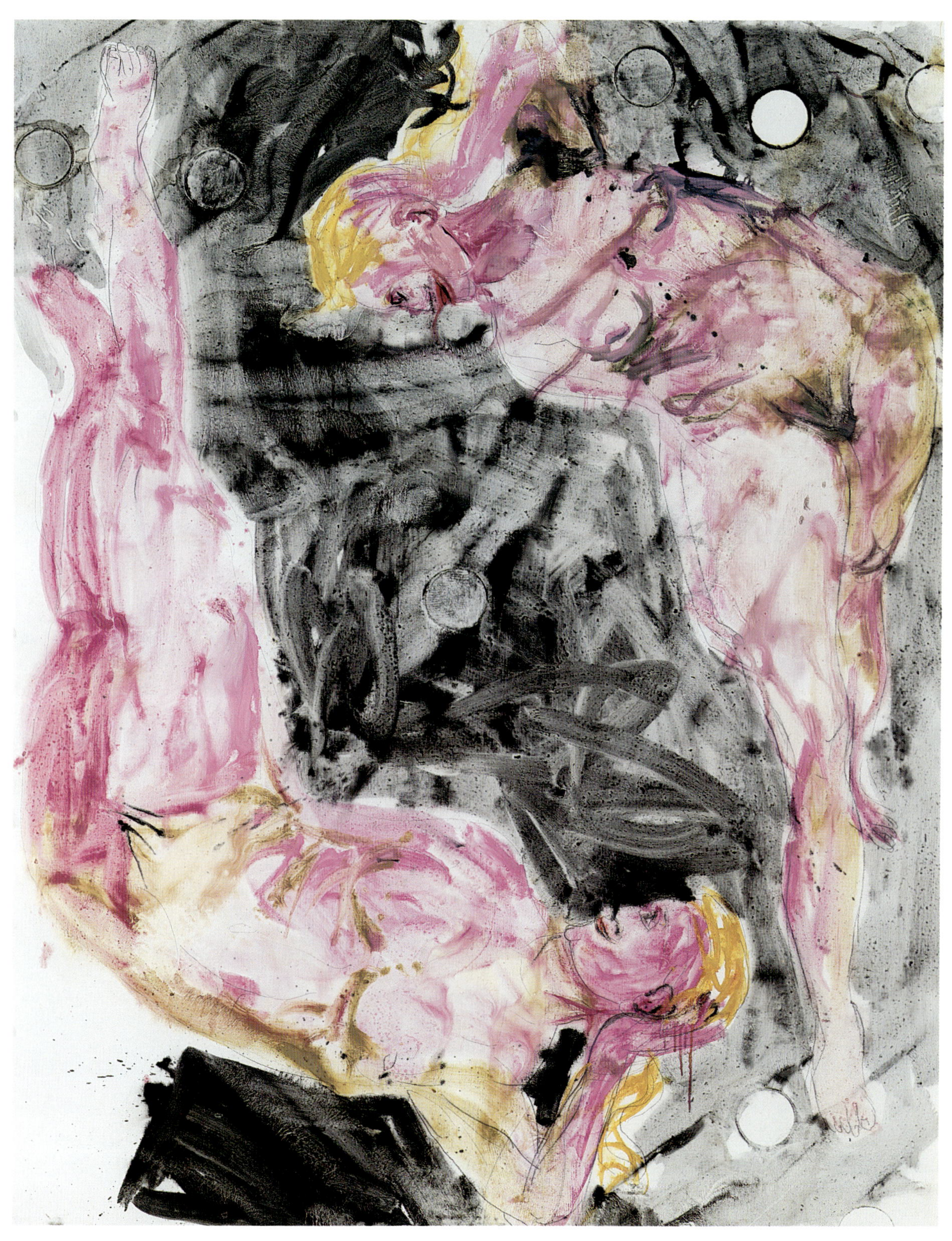

ADE NYMPHEN

June 17, 1998
oil on canvas, 82 x 63¾″

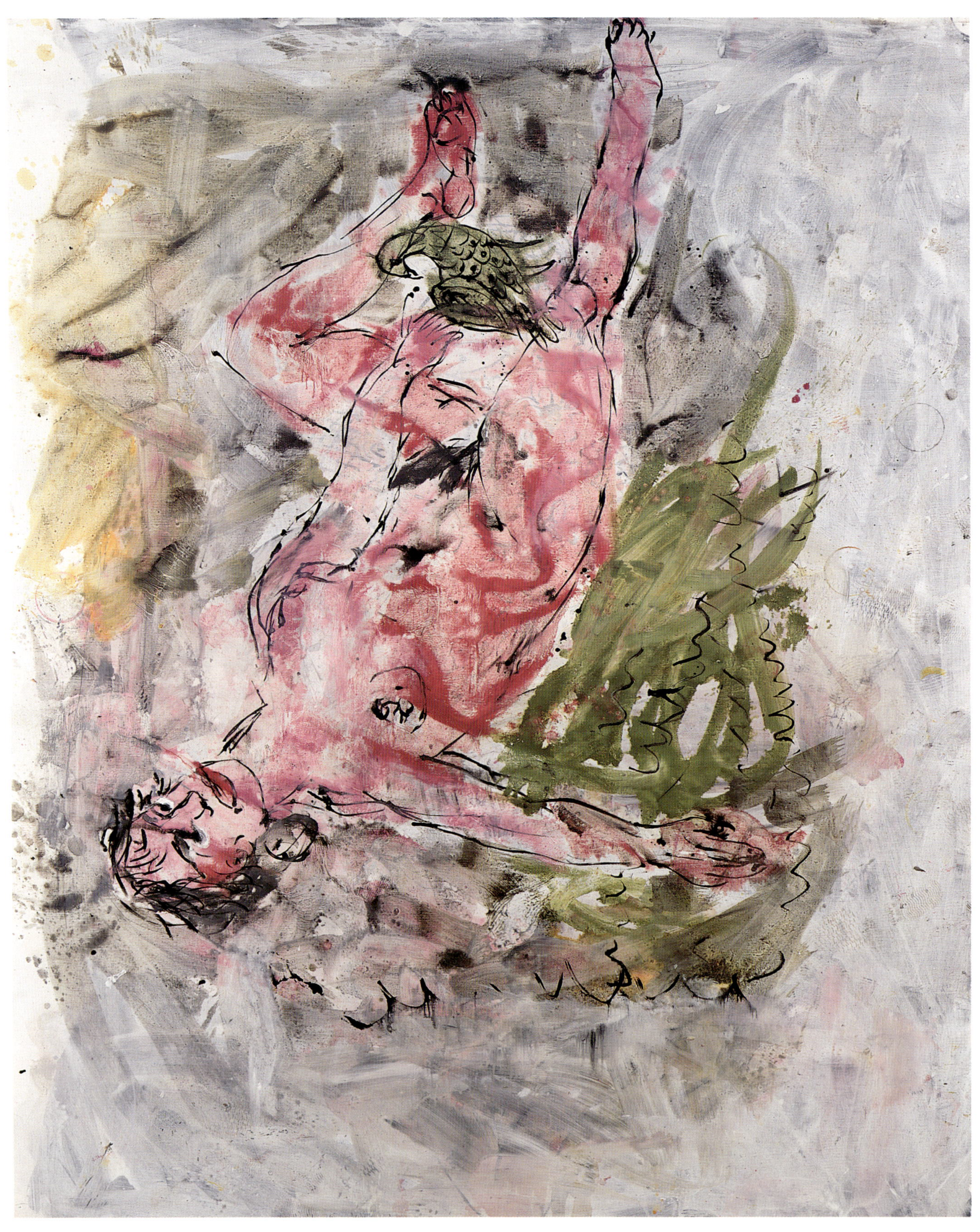

O'MURPHY SISTER

June 24, 1998
oil on canvas, 98 ½ x 78 ¾ ˝

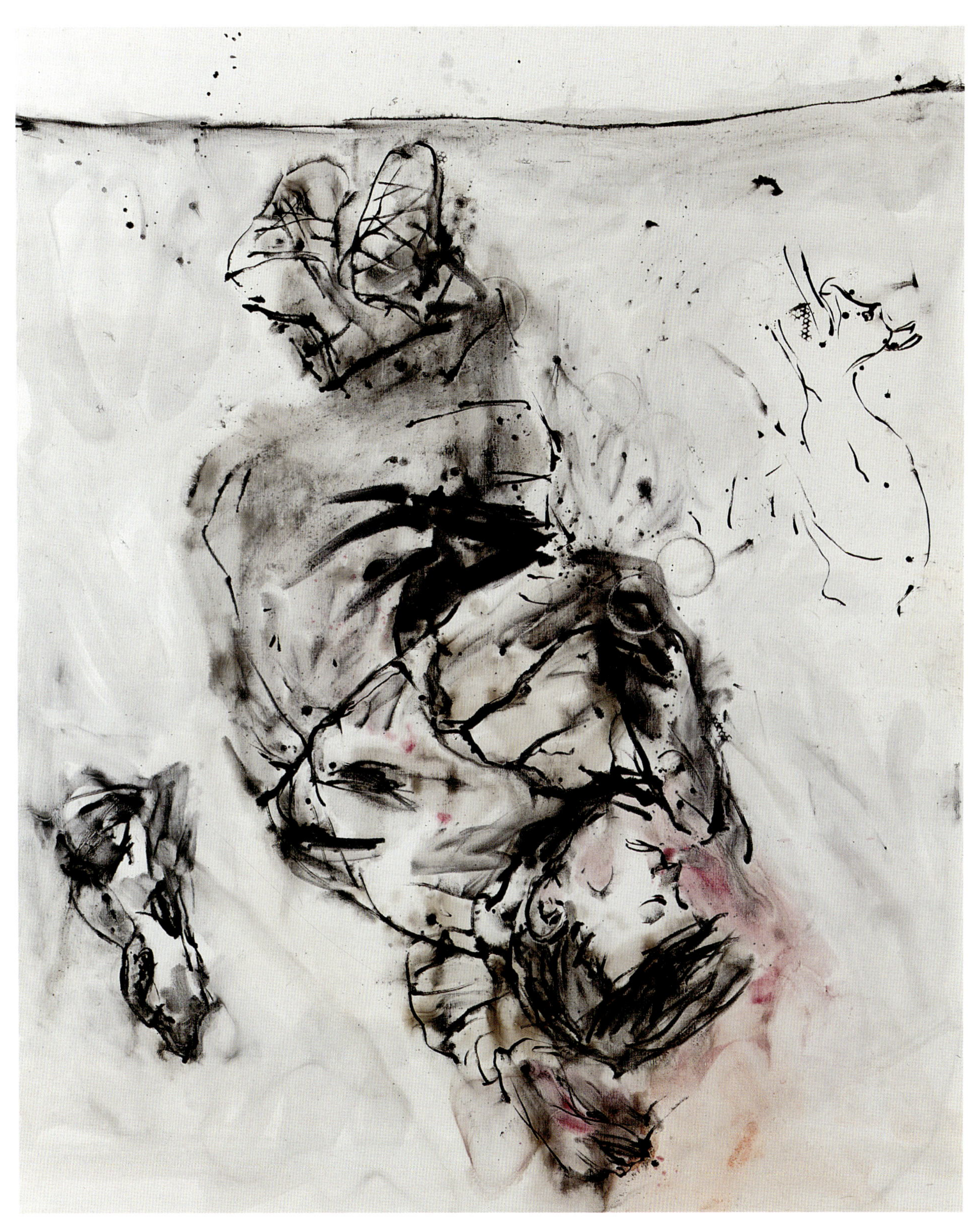

EIN FASCHIST FLOG VORÜBER III

July 17, 1998
oil on canvas, 80½ x 63¾˝

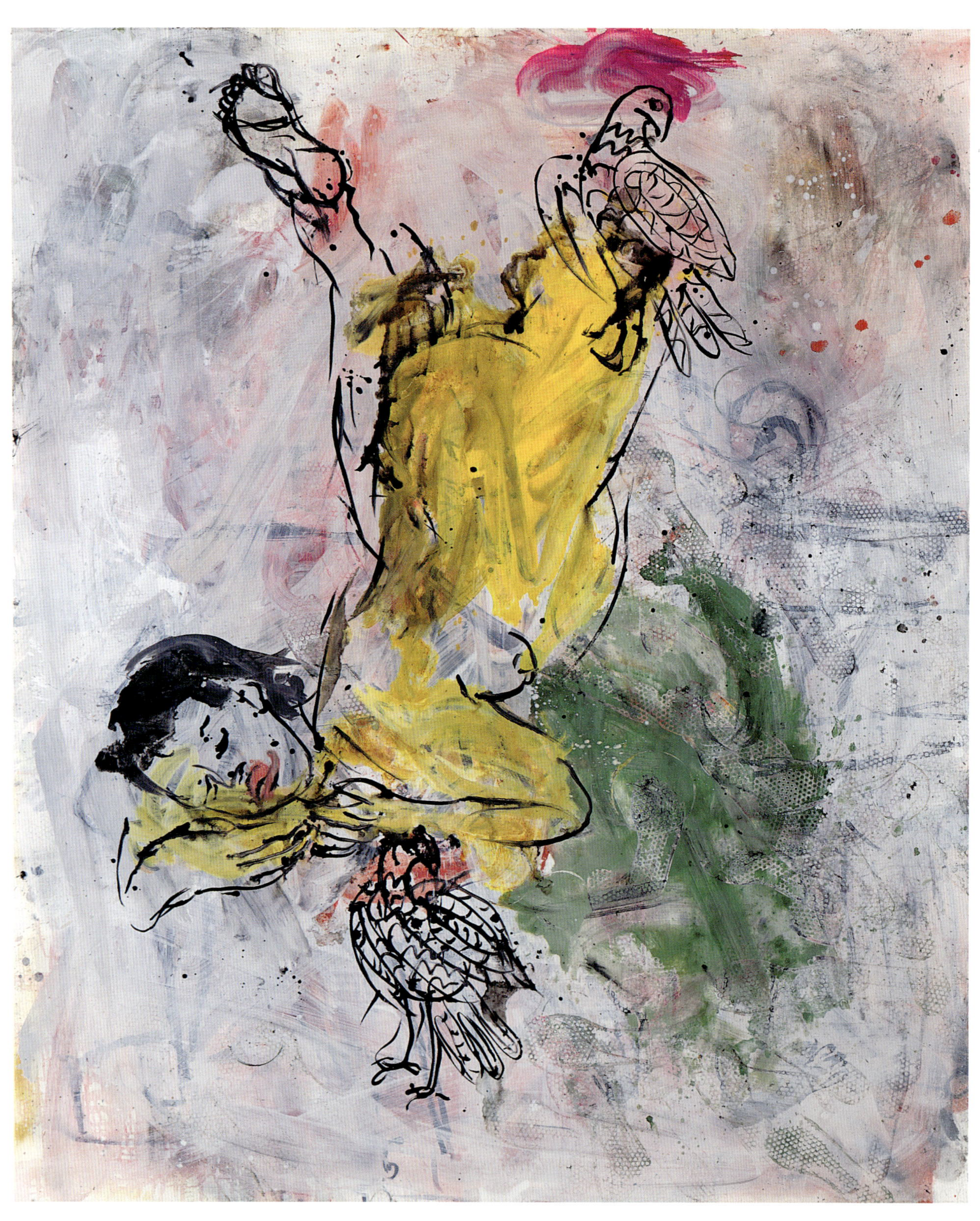

O'Murphy Sister II

July 22, 1998
oil on canvas, 80 ¼ x 65 ¼˝

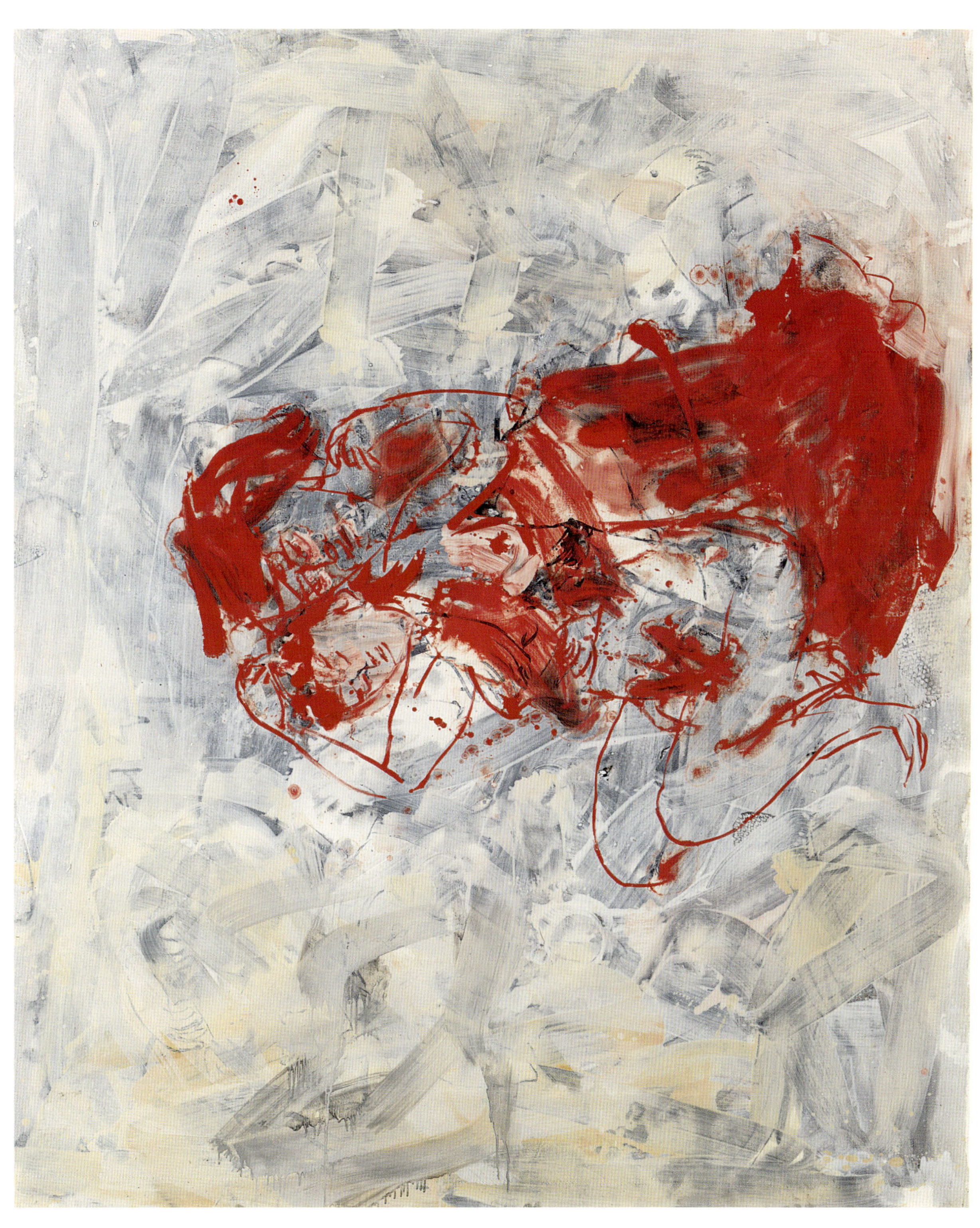

Persisches Liebespaar II

August 14, 1998
oil on canvas, 78¾ x 63¾″

CHECKLIST

Cover: PULLOVER OBEN, May 2-15, 1997, oil on canvas, 98½ x 78¾″ (detail)

Photography:
Martin Müller, page 4
Galerie Michael Werner, pages 13-27

Design and production:
Tomoko Makiura and Paul Pollard

ISBN: 1-878283-78-2